Alfred Tennyson

The Poetical Works of Alfred Tennyson - Gareth and Lynette

Alfred Tennyson

The Poetical Works of Alfred Tennyson - Gareth and Lynette

ISBN/EAN: 9783741163241

Manufactured in Europe, USA, Canada, Australia, Japa

Cover: Foto ©Andreas Hilbeck / pixelio.de

Manufactured and distributed by brebook publishing software (www.brebook.com)

Alfred Tennyson

The Poetical Works of Alfred Tennyson - Gareth and Lynette

EACH VOLUME SOLD SEPARATELY.

COLLECTION
OF
BRITISH AUTHORS

TAUCHNITZ EDITION.

VOL. 1277.

THE POETICAL WORKS OF TENNYSON

VOL. 7.

LEIPZIG: BERNHARD TAUCHNITZ.
PARIS: C. REINWALD & Cⁱᵉ, 15, RUE DES SAINTS PÈRES.

This Collection

COLLECTION
OF
BRITISH AUTHORS

TAUCHNITZ EDITION.

VOL. 1277.

THE POETICAL WORKS OF TENNYSON.

VOL. VII.

THE

POETICAL WORKS

OF

ALFRED TENNYSON.

COPYRIGHT EDITION.

VOL. VII.

GARETH AND LYNETTE;—THE LAST
TOURNAMENT.

LEIPZIG

BERNHARD TAUCHNITZ

1872.

OF these two Idylls, GARETH follows THE COMING OF ARTHUR, and THE LAST TOURNAMENT immediately precedes GUINEVERE.

GARETH AND LYNETTE.

GARETH AND LYNETTE.

THE last tall son of Lot and Bellicent,
And tallest, Gareth, in a showerful spring
Stared at the spate. A slender-shafted Pine
Lost footing, fell, and so was whirl'd away.
"How he went down," said Gareth, "as a false
    knight
Or evil king before my lance if lance
Were mine to use—O senseless cataract,
Bearing all down in thy precipitancy—
And yet thou art but swollen with cold snows,

And mine is living blood: thou dost His will,
The Maker's, and not knowest, and I that know,
Have strength and wit, in my good mother's hall
Linger with vacillating obedience,
Prison'd, and kept and coax'd and whistled
    to—
Since the good mother holds me still a child—
Good mother is bad mother unto me!
A worse were better; yet no worse would I
Heaven yield her for it, but in me put force
To weary her ears with one continuous prayer,
Until she let me fly discaged to sweep
In ever-highering eagle-circles up
To the great Sun of Glory, and thence swoop
Down upon all things base, and dash them
    dead,

A knight of Arthur, working out his will,
To cleanse the world. Why, Gawain, when he
    came
With Modred hither in the summertime,
Ask'd me to tilt with him, the proven knight.
Modred for want of worthier was the judge.
Then I so shook him in the saddle, he said,
'Thou hast half prevail'd against me,' said so—
    he—
Tho' Modred biting his thin lips was mute,
For he is alway sullen: what care I?"

    And Gareth went, and hovering round her
    chair
Ask'd, "Mother, tho' ye count me still the
    child,

Sweet mother, do ye love the child?" She laugh'd,
"Thou art but a wild-goose to question it."
"Then, mother, an ye love the child," he said,
"Being a goose and rather tame than wild,
Hear the child's story." "Yea, my well-beloved,
An 'twere but of the goose and golden eggs."

And Gareth answer'd her with kindling eyes,
"Nay, nay, good mother, but this egg of mine
Was finer gold than any goose can lay;
For this an Eagle, a royal Eagle, laid
Almost beyond eye-reach, on such a palm
As glitters gilded in thy Book of Hours.

And there was ever haunting round the palm
A lusty youth, but poor, who often saw
The splendour sparkling from aloft, and thought
'An I could climb and lay my hand upon it,
Then were I wealthier than a leash of kings.
But ever when he reach'd a hand to climb,
One, that had loved him from his childhood, caught
And stay'd him, 'Climb not lest thou break thy neck,
I charge thee by my love,' and so the boy,
Sweet mother, neither clomb, nor brake his neck,
But brake his very heart in pining for it,
And past away."

To whom the mother said,
"True love, sweet son, had risk'd himself and
  climb'd,
And handed down the golden treasure to him."

And Gareth answer'd her with kindling eyes,
"Gold? said I gold?—ay then, why he, or she,
Or whosoe'er it was, or half the world
Had ventured—*had* the thing I spake of been
Mere gold—but this was all of that true steel,
Whereof they forged the brand Excalibur,
And lightnings play'd about it in the storm,
And all the little fowl were flurried at it,
And there were cries and clashings in the nest,
That sent him from his senses: let me go."

Then Bellicent bemoan'd herself and said,
"Hast thou no pity upon my loneliness?
Lo, where thy father Lot beside the hearth
Lies like a log, and all but smoulder'd out!
For ever since when traitor to the King
He fought against him in the Barons' war,
And Arthur gave him back his territory,
His age hath slowly droopt, and now lies there
A yet-warm corpse, and yet unburiable,
No more; nor sees, nor hears, nor speaks, nor knows.
And both thy brethren are in Arthur's hall,
Albeit neither loved with that full love
I feel for thee, nor worthy such a love:
Stay therefore thou; red berries charm the bird,

And thee, mine innocent, the jousts, the wars,
Who never knewest finger-ache, nor pang
Of wrench'd or broken limb—an often chance
In those brain-stunning shocks, and tourney-
   falls,
Frights to my heart; but stay: follow the deer
By these tall firs and our fast-falling burns;
So make thy manhood mightier day by day;
Sweet is the chase: and I will seek thee out
Some comfortable bride and fair, to grace
Thy climbing life, and cherish my prone year,
Till falling into Lot's forgetfulness
I know not thee, myself, nor anything.
Stay, my best son! ye are yet more boy than
   man."

Then Gareth, "An ye hold me yet for
    child,
Hear yet once more the story of the child.
For, mother, there was once a King, like ours;
The prince his heir, when tall and marriageable,
Ask'd for a bride; and thereupon the King
Set two before him. One was fair, strong,
    arm'd—
But to be won by force—and many men
Desired her; one, good lack, no man desired.
And these were the conditions of the King:
That save he won the first by force, he needs
Must wed that other, whom no man desired,
A red-faced bride who knew herself so vile,
That evermore she long'd to hide herself,
Nor fronted man or woman, eye to eye—

Yea—some she cleaved to, but they died of
    her.
And one — they call'd her Fame; and one,
    O Mother,
How can ye keep me tether'd to you—Shame!
Man am I grown, a man's work must I do.
Follow the deer? follow the Christ, the King,
Live pure, speak true, right wrong, follow the
    King—
Else, wherefore born?"

       To whom the mother said,
"Sweet son, for there be many who deem him
    not,
Or will not deem him, wholly proven King—
Albeit in mine own heart I knew him King,

When I was frequent with him in my youth,
And heard him Kingly speak, and doubted him
No more than he, himself; but felt him mine,
Of closest kin to me: yet—wilt thou leave
Thine easeful biding here, and risk thine all,
Life, limbs, for one that is not proven King?
Stay, till the cloud that settles round his birth
Hath lifted but a little. Stay, sweet son."

And Gareth answer'd quickly, "Not an hour,
So that ye yield me—I will walk thro' fire,
Mother, to gain it—your full leave to go.
Not proven, who swept the dust of ruin'd Rome
From off the threshold of the realm, and crush'd

The Idolaters, and made the people free?
Who should be King save him who makes us
  free?"

  So when the Queen, who long had sought in
    vain
To break him from the intent to which he grew,
Found her son's will unwaveringly one,
She answer'd craftily, "Will ye walk thro'
  fire?
Who walks thro' fire will hardly heed the
  smoke.
Ay, go then, an ye must: only one proof,
Before thou ask the King to make thee knight,
Of thine obedience and thy love to me,
Thy mother,—I demand."

And Gareth cried,

"A hard one, or a hundred, so I go.

Nay—quick! the proof to prove me to the quick!"

But slowly spake the mother looking at him,

"Prince, thou shalt go disguised to Arthur's hall,

And hire thyself to serve for meats and drinks

Among the scullions and the kitchen-knaves,

And those that hand the dish across the bar.

Nor shalt thou tell thy name to anyone.

And thou shalt serve a twelvemonth and a day."

For so the Queen believed that when her son

Beheld his only way to glory lead

Low down thro' villain kitchen-vassalage,

Her own true Gareth was too princely-proud
To pass thereby; so should he rest with her,
Closed in her castle from the sound of arms.

    Silent awhile was Gareth, then replied.
"The thrall in person may be free in soul,
And I shall see the jousts. Thy son am I,
And since thou art my mother, must obey.
I therefore yield me freely to thy will;
For hence will I, disguised, and hire myself
To serve with scullions and with kitchen-
    knaves;
Nor tell my name to any—no, not the King."

    Gareth awhile linger'd. The mother's eye
Full of the wistful fear that he would go,

And turning toward him wheresoe'er he turn'd,
Perplext his outward purpose, till an hour,
When waken'd by the wind which with full
    voice
Swept bellowing thro' the darkness on to dawn,
He rose, and out of slumber calling two
That still had tended on him from his birth,
Before the wakeful mother heard him, went.

The three were clad like tillers of the soil.
Southward they set their faces. The birds
    made
Melody on branch, and melody in mid air.
The damp hill-slopes were quicken'd into green,
And the live green had kindled into flowers,
For it was past the time of Easterday.

So, when their feet were planted on the
    plain
That broaden'd toward the base of Camelot,
Far off they saw the silver-misty morn
Rolling her smoke about the Royal mount,
That rose between the forest and the field.
At times the summit of the high city flash'd;
At times the spires and turrets half-way down
Prick'd thro' the mist; at times the great gate
    shone
Only, that open'd on the field below:
Anon, the whole fair city had disappear'd.

    Then those who went with Gareth were
        amazed,
One crying, "Let us go no further, lord.

Here is a city of Enchanters, built
By fairy Kings." The second echo'd him,
"Lord, we have heard from our wise men at
    home
To Northward, that this King is not the King,
But only changeling out of Fairyland,
Who drave the heathen hence by sorcery
And Merlin's glamour." Then the first again,
"Lord, there is no such city anywhere,
But all a vision."

     Gareth answer'd them
With laughter, swearing he had glamour enow
In his own blood, his princedom, youth and
    hopes,
To plunge old Merlin in the Arabian sea;

So push'd them all unwilling toward the gate.
And there was no gate like it under heaven.
For barefoot on the keystone, which was lined
And rippled like an ever-fleeting wave,
The Lady of the Lake stood: all her dress
Wept from her sides as water flowing away;
But like the cross her great and goodly arms
Stretch'd under all the cornice and upheld:
And drops of water fell from either hand;
And down from one a sword was hung, from one
A censer, either worn with wind and storm;
And o'er her breast floated the sacred fish;
And in the space to left of her, and right,
Were Arthur's wars in weird devices done,
New things and old co-twisted, as if Time

Were nothing, so inveterately, that men
Were giddy gazing there; and over all
High on the top were those three Queens, the
    friends
Of Arthur, who should help him at his need.

Then those with Gareth for so long a space
Stared at the figures, that at last it seem'd
The dragon-boughts and elvish emblemings
Began to move, seethe, twine and curl: they
    call'd
To Gareth, "Lord, the gateway is alive."

And Gareth likewise on them fixt his eyes
So long, that ev'n to him they seem'd to move.
Out of the city a blast of music peal'd.

Back from the gate started the three, to whom
From out thereunder came an ancient man,
Long-bearded, saying, "Who be ye, my sons?"

Then Gareth, "We be tillers of the soil,
Who leaving share in furrow come to see
The glories of our King: but these, my men,
(Your city moved so weirdly in the mist)
Doubt if the King be King at all, or come
From fairyland; and whether this be built
By magic, and by fairy Kings and Queens;
Or whether there be any city at all,
Or all a vision: and this music now
Hath scared them both, but tell thou these the
      truth."

Then that old Seer made answer playing on
him
And saying, "Son, I have seen the good ship
sail
Keel upward and mast downward in the heavens,
And solid turrets topsy-turvy in air:
And here is truth; but an it please thee not,
Take thou the truth as thou hast told it me.
For truly, as thou sayest, a Fairy King
And Fairy Queens have built the city, son;
They came from out a sacred mountain-cleft
Toward the sunrise, each with harp in hand,
And built it to the music of their harps.
And as thou sayest it is enchanted, son,
For there is nothing in it as it seems
Saving the King; tho' some there be that hold

The King a shadow, and the city real:
Yet take thou heed of him, for, so thou pass
Beneath this archway, then wilt thou become
A thrall to his enchantments, for the King
Will bind thee by such vows, as is a shame
A man should not be bound by, yet the which
No man can keep; but, so thou dread to swear,
Pass not beneath this gateway, but abide
Without, among the cattle of the field.
For, an ye heard a music, like enow
They are building still, seeing the city is built
To music, therefore never built at all,
And therefore built for ever."

       Gareth spake
Anger'd, "Old Master, reverence thine own beard

That looks as white as utter truth, and seems
Wellnigh as long as thou art statured tall!
Why mockest thou the stranger that hath been
To thee fair-spoken?"

       But the Seer replied,
"Know ye not then the Riddling of the Bards?
"Confusion, and illusion, and relation,
Elusion, and occasion, and evasion"?
I mock thee not but as thou mockest me,
And all that see thee, for thou art not who
Thou seemest, but I know thee who thou art.
And now thou goest up to mock the King,
Who cannot brook the shadow of any lie."

Unmockingly the mocker ending here
Turn'd to the right, and past along the plain;
Whom Gareth looking after said, "My men,
Our one white lie sits like a little ghost
Here on the threshold of our enterprise.
Let love be blamed for it, not she, nor I:
Well, we will make amends."

                              With all good cheer
He spake and laugh'd, then enter'd with his
    twain
Camelot, a city of shadowy palaces
And stately, rich in emblem and the work
Of ancient kings who did their days in stone;
Which Merlin's hand, the Mage at Arthur's
    court,

Knowing all arts, had touch'd, and everywhere
At Arthur's ordinance, tipt with lessening peak
And pinnacle, and had made it spire to heaven.
And ever and anon a knight would pass
Outward, or inward to the hall: his arms
Clash'd; and the sound was good to Gareth's
    ear.
And out of bower and casement shyly glanced
Eyes of pure women, wholesome stars of love;
And all about a healthful people stept
As in the presence of a gracious king.

Then into hall Gareth ascending heard
A voice, the voice of Arthur, and beheld
Far over heads in that long-vaulted hall
The splendour of the presence of the King

Throned, and delivering doom—and look'd no more—
But felt his young heart hammering in his ears,
And thought, "For this half-shadow of a lie
The truthful King will doom me when I speak."
Yet pressing on, tho' all in fear to find
Sir Gawain or Sir Modred, saw nor one
Nor other, but in all the listening eyes
Of those tall knights, that ranged about the throne,
Clear honour shining like the dewy star
Of dawn, and faith in their great King, with pure
Affection, and the light of victory,
And glory gain'd, and evermore to gain.

Then came a widow crying to the King,
"A boon, Sir King! Thy father, Uther, reft
From my dead lord a field with violence:
For howsoe'er at first he proffer'd gold,
Yet, for the field was pleasant in our eyes,
We yielded not; and then he reft us of it
Perforce, and left us neither gold nor field."

Said Arthur, "Whether would ye? gold or
 field?"
To whom the woman weeping, "Nay, my lord,
The field was pleasant in my husband's eye."

And Arthur, "Have thy pleasant field again,
And thrice the gold for Uther's use thereof,
According to the years. No boon is here,

But justice, so thy say be proven true.
Accursed, who from the wrongs his father did
Would shape himself a right!"

      And while she past,
Came yet another widow crying to him,
"A boon, Sir King! Thine enemy, King, am I.
With thine own hand thou slewest my dear
  lord,
A knight of Uther in the Barons' war,
When Lot and many another rose and fought
Against thee, saying thou wert basely born.
I held with these, and loathe to ask thee aught.
Yet lo! my husband's brother had my son
Thrall'd in his castle, and hath starved him
  dead;

And standeth seized of that inheritance
Which thou that slewest the sire hast left the
	son,
So tho' I scarce can ask it thee for hate,
Grant me some knight to do the battle for me,
Kill the foul thief, and wreak me for my son."

Then strode a good knight forward, crying to
	him
"A boon, Sir King! I am her kinsman, I.
Give me to right her wrong, and slay the
	man."

Then came Sir Kay, the seneschal, and cried,
"A boon, Sir King! ev'n that thou grant her
	none,

This railer, that hath mock'd thee in full hall—
None; or the wholesome boon of gyve and
gag."

But Arthur, "We sit, King, to help the wrong'd
Thro' all our realm. The woman loves her lord.
Peace to thee, woman, with thy loves and hates!
The kings of old had doom'd thee to the flames,
Aurelius Emrys would have scourged thee dead,
And Uther slit thy tongue: but get thee hence —
Lest that rough humour of the kings of old

Return upon me! Thou that art her kin,
Go likewise; lay him low and slay him not,
But bring him here, that I may judge the right,
According to the justice of the King:
Then, be he guilty, by that deathless King
Who lived and died for men, the man shall
    die."

Then came in hall the messenger of Mark,
A name of evil savour in the land,
The Cornish king. In either hand he bore
What dazzled all, and shone far-off as shines
A field of charlock in the sudden sun
Between two showers, a cloth of palest gold,
Which down he laid before the throne, and
    knelt,

Delivering, that his lord, the vassal king,
Was ev'n upon his way to Camelot;
For having heard that Arthur of his grace
Had made his goodly cousin, Tristram, knight,
And, for himself was of the greater state,
Being a king, he trusted his liege-lord
Would yield him this large honour all the
 more;
So pray'd him well to accept this cloth of
 gold,
In token of true heart and feälty.

Then Arthur cried to rend the cloth, to rend
In pieces, and so cast it on the hearth.
An oak-tree smoulder'd there. "The goodly
 knight!

What! shall the shield of Mark stand among
    these?"
For, midway down the side of that long hall
A stately pile,—whereof along the front,
Some blazon'd, some but carven, and some
    blank,
There ran a treble range of stony shields,—
Rose, and high-arching overbrow'd the hearth.
And under every shield a knight was named:
For this was Arthur's custom in his hall;
When some good knight had done one noble
    deed,
His arms were carven only; but if twain
His arms were blazon'd also; but if none
The shield was blank and bare without a sign
Saving the name beneath; and Gareth saw

The shield of Gawain blazon'd rich and bright,
And Modred's blank as death; and Arthur cried
To rend the cloth and cast it on the hearth.

"More like are we to reave him of his crown
Than make him knight because men call him
        king.
The kings we found, ye know we stay'd their
        hands
From war among themselves, but left them
        kings;
Of whom were any bounteous, merciful,
Truth-speaking, brave, good livers, them we
        enroll'd
Among us, and they sit within our hall.
But Mark hath tarnish'd the great name of king,

As Mark would sully the low state of churl:
And, seeing he hath sent us cloth of gold,
Return, and meet, and hold him from our eyes,
Lest we should lap him up in cloth of lead,
Silenced for ever—craven—a man of plots,
Craft, poisonous counsels, wayside ambushings—
No fault of thine: let Kay the seneschal
Look to thy wants, and send thee satisfied—
Accursed, who strikes nor lets the hand be seen!"

And many another suppliant crying came
With noise of ravage wrought by beast and man,
And evermore a knight would ride away.

Last Gareth leaning both hands heavily
Down on the shoulders of the twain, his men,
Approach'd between them toward the King, and
                    ask'd,
"A boon, Sir King (his voice was all ashamed),
For see ye not how weak and hungerworn
I seem—leaning on these? grant me to serve
For meat and drink among thy kitchen-knaves
A twelvemonth and a day, nor seek my name.
Hereafter I will fight."

                            To him the King,
"A goodly youth and worth a goodlier boon!
But an thou wilt no goodlier, then must Kay,
The master of the meats and drinks, be thine."

He rose and past; then Kay, a man of mien
Wan-sallow as the plant that feels itself
Root-bitten by white lichen,

"Lo ye now!
This fellow hath broken from some Abbey,
where,
God wot, he had not beef and brewis enow,
However that might chance! but an he work,
Like any pigeon will I cram his crop,
And sleeker shall he shine than any hog."

Then Lancelot standing near, "Sir Seneschal,
Sleuth-hound thou knowest, and gray, and all the
hounds;
A horse thou knowest, a man thou dost not
know:

Broad brows and fair, a fluent hair and fine,
High nose, a nostril large and fine, and hands
Large, fair and fine!—Some young lad's
    mystery—
But, or from sheepcot or king's hall, the boy
Is noble-natured. Treat him with all grace,
Lest he should come to shame thy judging of
    him."

Then Kay, "What murmurest thou of mystery?
Think ye this fellow will poison the King's
    dish?
Nay, for he spake too fool-like: mystery!
Tut, an the lad were noble, he had ask'd
For horse and armour: fair and fine, forsooth!
Sir Fine-face, Sir Fair-hands! but see thou to it

That thine own fineness, Lancelot, some fine
day
Undo thee not — and leave my man to me."

So Gareth all for glory underwent
The sooty yoke of kitchen vassalage;
Ate with young lads his portion by the door,
And couch'd at night with grimy kitchen-
knaves.
And Lancelot ever spake him pleasantly,
But Kay the seneschal who loved him not
Would hustle and harry him, and labour him
Beyond his comrade of the hearth, and set
To turn the broach, draw water, or hew wood,
Or grosser tasks; and Gareth bow'd himself
With all obedience to the King, and wrought

All kind of service with a noble ease
That graced the lowliest act in doing it.
And when the thralls had talk among them-
    selves,
And one would praise the love that linkt the
    King
And Lancelot—how the King had saved his life
In battle twice, and Lancelot once the King's—
For Lancelot was the first in Tournament,
But Arthur mightiest on the battlefield—
Gareth was glad. Or if some other told,
How once the wandering forester at dawn,
Far over the blue tarns and hazy seas,
On Caer-Eryri's highest found the King,
A naked babe, of whom the Prophet spake,
"He passes to the Isle Avilion,

He passes and is heal'd and cannot die"—
Gareth was glad. But if their talk were foul,
Then would he whistle rapid as any lark,
Or carol some old roundelay, and so loud
That first they mock'd, but, after, reverenced
    him.
Or Gareth telling some prodigious tale
Of knights, who sliced a red life-bubbling way
Thro' twenty folds of twisted dragon, held
All in a gap-mouth'd circle his good mates
Lying or sitting round him, idle hands,
Charm'd; till Sir Kay, the seneschal, would
    come
Blustering upon them, like a sudden wind
Among dead leaves, and drive them all apart.
Or when the thralls had sport among themselves,

So there were any trial of mastery,
He, by two yards in casting bar or stone
Was counted best; and if there chanced a joust,
So that Sir Kay nodded him leave to go,
Would hurry thither, and when he saw the knights
Clash like the coming and retiring wave,
And the spear spring, and good horse reel, the boy
Was half beyond himself for ecstasy.

So for a month he wrought among the thralls;
But in the weeks that follow'd, the good Queen,

Repentant of the word she made him swear,
And saddening in her childless castle, sent,
Between the increscent and decrescent moon,
Arms for her son, and loosed him from his
    vow.

This, Gareth hearing from a squire of Lot
With whom he used to play at tourney once,
When both were children, and in lonely haunts
Would scratch a ragged oval on the sand,
And each at either dash from either end—
Shame never made girl redder than Gareth
    joy.
He laugh'd; he sprang. "Out of the smoke, at
    once
I leap from Satan's foot to Peter's knee—

These news be mine, none other's—nay, the
    King's—
Descend into the city:" whereon he sought
The King alone, and found, and told him all.

"I have stagger'd thy strong Gawain in a
    tilt
For pastime; yea, he said it: joust can I.
Make me thy knight—in secret! let my name
Be hidd'n, and give me the first quest, I spring
Like flame from ashes."

               Here the King's calm eye
Fell on, and check'd, and made him flush, and
    bow
Lowly, to kiss his hand, who answer'd him,

"Son, the good mother let me know thee
       here,
And sent her wish that I would yield thee
       thine.
Make thee my knight? my knights are sworn to
       vows
Of utter hardihood, utter gentleness,
And, loving, utter faithfulness in love,
And uttermost obedience to the King."

    Then Gareth, lightly springing from his
       knees,
"My King, for hardihood I can promise thee.
For uttermost obedience make demand
Of whom ye gave me to, the Seneschal,
No mellow master of the meats and drinks!

And as for love, God wot, I love not yet,
But love I shall, God willing."

                        And the King—
"Make thee my knight in secret? yea, but he,
Our noblest brother, and our truest man,
And one with me in all, he needs must know."

  "Let Lancelot know, my King, let Lancelot
            know,
Thy noblest and thy truest!"

                        And the King—
"But wherefore would ye men should wonder at
            you?
Nay, rather for the sake of me, their King,

And the deed's sake my knighthood do the
    deed,
Than to be noised of."

                    Merrily Gareth ask'd,
"Have I not earn'd my cake in baking of it?
Let be my name until I make my name!
My deeds will speak: it is but for a day."
So with a kindly hand on Gareth's arm
Smiled the great King, and half-unwillingly
Loving his lusty youthhood yielded to him.
Then, after summoning Lancelot privily,
"I have given him the first quest: he is not
    proven.
Look therefore when he calls for this in hall,
Thou get to horse and follow him far away.

Cover the lions on thy shield, and see
Far as thou mayest; he be nor ta'en nor slain."

Then that same day there past into the hall
A damsel of high lineage, and a brow
May-blossom, and a cheek of apple-blossom,
Hawk-eyes; and lightly was her slender nose
Tip-tilted like the petal of a flower;
She into hall past with her page and cried,

"O King, for thou hast driven the foe
without,
See to the foe within! bridge, ford, beset
By bandits, everyone that owns a tower
The Lord for half a league. Why sit ye
there?

Rest would I not, Sir King, an I were king,
Till ev'n the lonest hold were all as free
From cursed bloodshed, as thine altar-cloth
From that blest blood it is a sin to spill."

"Comfort thyself," said Arthur, "I nor mine
Rest: so my knighthood keep the vows they
    swore,
The wastest moorland of our realm shall be
Safe, damsel, as the centre of this hall.
What is thy name? thy need?"

"My name?" she said—
"Lynette my name; noble; my need, a
    knight
To combat for my sister, Lyonors,

A lady of high lineage, of great lands,
And comely, yea, and comelier than myself.
She lives in Castle Perilous: a river
Runs in three loops about her living-place;
And o'er it are three passings, and three
    knights
Defend the passings, brethren, and a fourth
And of that four the mightiest, holds her
    stay'd
In her own castle and so besieges her
To break her will, and make her wed with
    him:
And but delays his purport till thou send
To do the battle with him, thy chief man
Sir Lancelot whom he trusts to overthrow,
Then wed, with glory; but she will not wed

Save whom she loveth, or a holy life.
Now therefore have I come for Lancelot."

Then Arthur mindful of Sir Gareth ask'd,
"Damsel, ye know this Order lives to crush
All wrongers of the Realm. But say, these four,
Who be they? What the fashion of the men?"

"They be of foolish fashion, O Sir King,
The fashion of that old knight-errantry
Who ride abroad and do but what they will;
Courteous or bestial from the moment, such
As have nor law nor king; and three of these

Proud in their fantasy call themselves the Day,
Morning-Star, and Noon-Sun, and Evening-Star,
Being strong fools; and never a whit more wise
The fourth, who alway rideth arm'd in black,
A huge man-beast of boundless savagery.
He names himself the Night and oftener Death —
And wears a helmet mounted with a skull,
And bears a skeleton figured on his arms,
To show that who may slay or scape the three
Slain by himself shall enter endless night.
And all these four be fools, but mighty men,
And therefore am I come for Lancelot."

Hereat Sir Gareth call'd from where he
rose,
A head with kindling eyes above the throng,
"A boon, Sir King—this quest!" then—for he
mark'd
Kay near him groaning like a wounded bull—
"Yea, King, thou knowest thy kitchen-knave
am I,
And mighty thro' thy meats and drinks am I,
And I can topple over a hundred such.
Thy promise, King," and Arthur glancing at
him,
Brought down a momentary brow. "Rough,
sudden,
And pardonable, worthy to be knight—
Go therefore," and all hearers were amazed.

But on the damsel's forehead shame, pride, wrath
Slew the May-white: she lifted either arm,
"Fie on thee, King! I ask'd for thy chief knight,
And thou hast given me but a kitchen-knave."
Then ere a man in hall could stay her, turn'd,
Fled down the lane of access to the King,
Took horse, descended the slope street, and past
The weird white gate, and paused without, beside
The field of tourney, murmuring "kitchen-knave."

GARETH AND LYNETTE.

Now two great entries open'd from the hall,
At one end one, that gave upon a range
Of level pavement where the King would pace
At sunrise, gazing over plain and wood.
And down from this a lordly stairway sloped
Till lost in blowing trees and tops of towers.
And out by this main doorway past the King.
But one was counter to the hearth, and rose
High that the highest-crested helm could ride
Therethro' nor graze: and by this entry fled
The damsel in her wrath, and on to this
Sir Gareth strode, and saw without the door
King Arthur's gift, the worth of half a town,
A warhorse of the best, and near it stood
The two that out of north had follow'd him:
This bare a maiden shield, a casque; that held

The horse, the spear; whereat Sir Gareth
    loosed
A cloak that dropt from collar-bone to heel,
A cloth of roughest web, and cast it down,
And from it like a fuel-smother'd fire,
That lookt half-dead, brake bright, and flash'd
    as those
Dull-coated things, that making slide apart
Their dusk wing-cases, all beneath there burns
A jewell'd harness, ere they pass and fly.
So Gareth ere he parted flash'd in arms.
Then while he donn'd the helm, and took the
    shield
And mounted horse and graspt a spear, of
    grain
Storm-strengthen'd on a windy site, and tipt

With trenchant steel, around him slowly prest
The people, and from out of kitchen came
The thralls in throng, and seeing who had
    work'd
Lustier than any, and whom they could but
    love,
Mounted in arms, threw up their caps and
    cried,
"God bless the King, and all his fellowship!"
And on thro' lanes of shouting Gareth rode
Down the slope street, and past without the
    gate.

So Gareth past with joy; but as the cur
Pluckt from the cur he fights with, ere his
    cause

Be cool'd by fighting, follows, being named,
His owner, but remembers all, and growls
Remembering, so Sir Kay beside the door
Mutter'd in scorn of Gareth whom he used
To harry and hustle.

"Bound upon a quest
With horse and arms—the King hath past his
    time—
My scullion knave! Thralls to your work
    again,
For an your fire be low ye kindle mine!
Will there be dawn in West and eve in East?
Begone!—my knave!—belike and like enow
Some old head-blow not heeded in his youth
So shook his wits they wander in his prime—

Crazed! How the villain lifted up his voice,
Nor shamed to bawl himself a kitchen-knave.
Tut: he was tame and meek enow with me,
Till peacock'd up with Lancelot's noticing.
Well—I will after my loud knave, and learn
Whether he know me for his master yet.
Out of the smoke he came, and so my lance
Hold, by God's grace, he shall into the mire—
Thence, if the King awaken from his craze,
Into the smoke again."

But Lancelot said,
"Kay, wherefore will ye go against the King,
For that did never he whereon ye rail,
But ever meekly served the King in thee?
Abide: take counsel for this lad is great

And lusty, and knowing both of lance and
  sword."
"Tut, tell not me," said Kay, "ye are overfine
To mar stout knaves with foolish courtesies."
Then mounted, on thro' silent faces rode
Down the slope city, and out beyond the gate.

 But by the field of tourney lingering yet
Mutter'd the damsel, "Wherefore did the King
Scorn me? for, were Sir Lancelot lackt, at
  least
He might have yielded to me one of those
Who tilt for lady's love and glory here,
Rather than—O sweet heaven! O fie upon
  him—
His kitchen-knave."

To whom Sir Gareth drew
(And there were none but few goodlier than he)
Shining in arms, "Damsel, the quest is mine.
Lead, and I follow." She thereat, as one
That smells a foul-flesh'd agaric in the holt,
And deems it carrion of some woodland thing,
Or shrew, or weasel, nipt her slender nose
With petulant thumb and finger, shrilling
"Hence!
Avoid, thou smellest all of kitchen-grease.
And look who comes behind," for there was
Kay.
"Knowest thou not me? thy master? I am
Kay.
We lack thee by the hearth."

And Gareth to him,
"Master no more! too well I know thee, ay—
The most ungentle knight in Arthur's hall."
"Have at thee then," said Kay: they shock'd,
and Kay
Fell shoulder-slipt, and Gareth cried again,
"Lead, and I follow," and fast away she fled.

But after sod and shingle ceased to fly
Behind her, and the heart of her good horse
Was nigh to burst with violence of the beat,
Perforce she stay'd, and overtaken spoke.

"What doest thou, scullion, in my fellow-
    ship?
Deem'st thou that I accept thee aught the more

Or love thee better, that by some device
Full cowardly, or by mere unhappiness,
Thou hast overthrown and slain thy master—
   thou!—
Dish-washer and broach-turner, loon!—to me
Thou smellest all of kitchen as before."

"Damsel," Sir Gareth answer'd gently, "say
Whate'er ye will, but whatsoe'er ye say,
I leave not till I finish this fair quest,
Or die therefore."

            "Ay, wilt thou finish it?
Sweet lord, how like a noble knight he talks!
The listening rogue hath caught the manner
   of it.

But, knave, anon thou shalt be met with,
	knave,
And then by such a one that thou for all
The kitchen brewis that was ever supt
Shalt not once dare to look him in the face."

"I shall assay," said Gareth with a smile
That madden'd her, and away she flash'd
	again
Down the long avenues of a boundless wood,
And Gareth following was again beknaved.

"Sir Kitchen-knave, I have miss'd the only
	way
Where Arthur's men are set along the wood;
The wood is nigh as full of thieves as leaves:

If both be slain, I am rid of thee; but yet,
Sir Scullion, canst thou use that spit of
    thine?
Fight, an thou canst: I have miss'd the only
    way."

So till the dusk that follow'd evensong
Rode on the two, reviler and reviled;
Then after one long slope was mounted,
    saw,
Bowl-shaped, thro' tops of many thousand
    pines
A gloomy-gladed hollow slowly sink
To westward—in the deeps whereof a mere,
Round as the red eye of an Eagle-owl,
Under the half-dead sunset glared; and shouts

Ascended, and there brake a servingman
Flying from out of the black wood, and
 crying,
"They have bound my lord to cast him in the
 mere."
Then Gareth, "Bound am I to right the
 wrong'd,
But straitlier bound am I to bide with thee."
And when the damsel spake contemptuously,
"Lead and I follow," Gareth cried again,
"Follow, I lead!" so down among the pines
He plunged; and there, blackshadow'd nigh the
 mere,
And mid-thigh-deep in bulrushes and reed,
Saw six tall men haling a seventh along,
A stone about his neck to drown him in it.

Three with good blows he quieted, but three
Fled thro' the pines; and Gareth loosed the stone
From off his neck, then in the mere beside
Tumbled it; oilily bubbled up the mere.
Last, Gareth loosed his bonds and on free feet
Set him, a stalwart Baron, Arthur's friend.

"Well that ye came, or else these caitiff rogues
Had wreak'd themselves on me; good cause is theirs
To hate me, for my wont hath ever been
To catch my thief, and then like vermin here
Drown him, and with a stone about his neck;

And under this wan water many of them
Lie rotting, but at night let go the stone,
And rise, and flickering in a grimly light
Dance on the mere. Good now, ye have saved
   a life
Worth somewhat as the cleanser of this wood.
And fain would I reward thee worshipfully.
What guerdon will ye?"

        Gareth sharply spake,
"None! for the deed's sake have I done the deed,
In uttermost obedience to the King.
But will ye yield this damsel harbourage?"

 Whereat the Baron saying, "I well believe
Ye be of Arthur's Table," a light laugh

Broke from Lynette, "Ay, truly of a truth,
And in a sort, being Arthur's kitchen-knave!—
But deem not I accept thee aught the more,
Scullion, for running sharply with thy spit
Down on a rout of craven foresters.
A thresher with his flail had scatter'd them.
Nay—for thou smellest of the kitchen still.
But an this lord will yield us harbourage,
Well."

So she spake. A league beyond the wood,
All in a full-fair manor and a rich,
His towers where that day a feast had been
Held in high hall, and many a viand left,
And many a costly cate, received the three.

And there they placed a peacock in his pride
Before the damsel, and the Baron set
Gareth beside her, but at once she rose.

"Meseems, that here is much discourtesy,
Setting this knave, Lord Baron, at my side.
Hear me—this morn I stood in Arthur's hall,
And pray'd the King would grant me Lancelot
To fight the brotherhood of Day and Night—
The last a monster unsubduable
Of any save of him for whom I call'd—
Suddenly bawls this frontless kitchen-knave,
'The quest is mine; thy kitchen-knave am I,
And mighty thro' thy meats and drinks am I.'
Then Arthur all at once gone mad replies,
'Go therefore,' and so gives the quest to him—

Him—here—a villain fitter to stick swine
Than ride abroad redressing women's wrong,
Or sit beside a noble gentlewoman."

Then half-ashamed and part-amazed, the lord
Now look'd at one and now at other, left
The damsel by the peacock in his pride,
And, seating Gareth at another board,
Sat down beside him, ate and then began.

"Friend, whether ye be kitchen-knave, or not,
Or whether it be the maiden's fantasy,
And whether she be mad, or else the King,
Or both or neither, or thyself be mad,
I ask not: but thou strikest a strong stroke,
For strong thou art and goodly therewithal,

And saver of my life; and therefore now,
For here be mighty men to joust with, weigh
Whether thou wilt not with thy damsel back
To crave again Sir Lancelot of the King.
Thy pardon; I but speak for thine avail,
The saver of my life."

                    And Gareth said,
"Full pardon, but I follow up the quest,
Despite of Day and Night and Death and
    Hell."

    So when, next morn, the lord whose life he
        saved
Had, some brief space, convey'd them on their
        way

And left them with God-speed, Sir Gareth,
spake,
"Lead and I follow." Haughtily she replied,

"I fly no more: I allow thee for an hour.
Lion and stoat have isled together, knave,
In time of flood. Nay, furthermore, methinks
Some ruth is mine for thee. Back wilt thou,
fool?
For hard by here is one will overthrow
And slay thee: then will I to court again,
And shame the King for only yielding me
My champion from the ashes of his hearth."

To whom Sir Gareth answer'd courteously,
"Say thou thy say, and I will do my deed.

Allow me for mine hour, and thou wilt find
My fortunes all as fair as hers, who lay
Among the ashes and wedded the King's son."

Then to the shore of one of those long
    loops
Wherethro' the serpent river coil'd, they came.
Rough-thicketed were the banks and steep; the
    stream
Full, narrow; this a bridge of single arc
Took at a leap; and on the further side
Arose a silk pavilion, gay with gold
In streaks and rays, and all Lent-lily in hue,
Save that the dome was purple, and above,
Crimson, a slender banneret fluttering.
And therebefore the lawless warrior paced

Unarm'd, and calling, "Damsel, is this he,
The champion ye have brought from Arthur's
    hall,
For whom we let thee pass?" "Nay, nay," she
    said,
"Sir Morning-Star. The King in utter scorn
Of thee and thy much folly hath sent thee here
His kitchen-knave: and look thou to thyself:
See that he fall not on thee suddenly,
And slay thee unarm'd: he is not knight but
    knave."

Then at his call, "O daughters of the Dawn,
And servants of the Morning-Star, approach,
Arm me," from out the silken curtain-folds
Bare-footed and bare-headed three fair girls

In gilt and rosy raiment came: their feet
In dewy grasses glisten'd; and the hair
All over glanced with dewdrop or with gem
Like sparkles in the stone Avanturine.
These arm'd him in blue arms, and gave a
shield
Blue also, and thereon the morning star.
And Gareth silent gazed upon the knight,
Who stood a moment, ere his horse was
brought,
Glorying; and in the stream beneath him,
shone,
Immingled with Heaven's azure waveringly,
The gay pavilion and the naked feet,
His arms, the rosy raiment, and the star.

Then she that watch'd him, "Wherefore stare
 ye so?
Thou shakest in thy fear: there yet is time:
Flee down the valley before he get to horse.
Who will cry shame? Thou art not knight but
 knave."

Said Gareth, "Damsel, whether knave or
 knight,
Far liefer had I fight a score of times
Than hear thee so missay me and revile.
Fair words were best for him who fights for
 thee;
But truly foul are better, for they send
That strength of anger thro' mine arms, I know
That I shall overthrow him."

And he that bore
The star, being mounted, cried from o'er the
bridge,
"A kitchen-knave, and sent in scorn of me!
Such fight not I, but answer scorn with scorn.
For this were shame to do him further wrong
Than set him on his feet, and take his horse
And arms, and so return him to the King.
Come, therefore, leave thy lady lightly, knave.
Avoid: for it beseemeth not a knave
To ride with such a lady."

"Dog, thou liest.
I spring from loftier lineage than thine own."
He spake; and all at fiery speed the two
Shock'd on the central bridge, and either spear

Bent but not brake, and either knight at
    once,
Hurl'd as a stone from out of a catapult
Beyond his horse's crupper and the bridge,
Fell, as if dead; but quickly rose and drew,
And Gareth lash'd so fiercely with his
    brand
He drave his enemy backward down the
    bridge,
The damsel crying, "Well-stricken, kitchen-
    knave!"
Till Gareth's shield was cloven; but one
    stroke
Laid him that clove it grovelling on the
    ground.

Then cried the fall'n, "Take not my life:
    I yield."
And Gareth, "So this damsel ask it of me
Good—I accord it easily as a grace."
She reddening, "Insolent scullion: I of thee?
I bound to thee for any favour ask'd!"
"Then shall he die." And Gareth there un-
    laced
His helmet as to slay him, but she shriek'd,
"Be not so hardy, scullion, as to slay
One nobler than thyself." "Damsel, thy charge
Is an abounding pleasure to me. Knight,
Thy life is thine at her command. Arise
And quickly pass to Arthur's hall, and say
His kitchen-knave hath sent thee. See thou
    crave

His pardon for thy breaking of his laws.
Myself, when I return, will plead for thee.
Thy shield is mine—farewell; and, damsel,
    thou,
Lead, and I follow."

                    And fast away she fled.
Then when he came upon her, spake, "Me-
    thought,
Knave, when I watch'd thee striking on the
    bridge
The savour of thy kitchen came upon me
A little faintlier: but the wind hath changed:
I scent it twentyfold." And then she sang,
"'O morning star' (not that tall felon there
Whom thou by sorcery or unhappiness

Or some device, hast foully overthrown),
'O morning star that smilest in the blue,
O star, my morning dream hath proven true,
Smile sweetly, thou! my love hath smiled on
    me.'

"But thou begone, take counsel, and away,
For hard by here is one that guards a ford—
The second brother in their fool's parable
Will pay thee all thy wages, and to boot.
Care not for shame: thou art not knight but
    knave."

To whom Sir Gareth answer'd, laughingly,
"Parables? Hear a parable of the knave.
When I was kitchen-knave among the rest

Fierce was the hearth, and one of my co-
mates
Own'd a rough dog, to whom he cast his
coat,
'Guard it,' and there was none to meddle
with it.
And such a coat art thou, and thee the
King
Gave me to guard, and such a dog am I,
To worry, and not to flee—and—knight or
knave—
The knave that doth thee service as full
knight
Is all as good, meseems, as any knight
Toward thy sister's freeing."

"Ay, Sir Knave!
Ay, knave, because thou strikest as a knight,
Being but knave, I hate thee all the more."

"Fair damsel, ye should worship me the
    more,
That, being but knave, I throw thine enemies."

"Ay, ay," she said, "but thou shalt meet thy
    match."

So when they touch'd the second river-
    loop,
Huge on a huge red horse, and all in mail
Burnish'd to blinding, shone the Noonday Sun
Beyond a raging shallow. As if the flower,

That blows a globe of after arrowlets,
Ten thousand-fold had grown, flash'd the fierce
 shield,
All sun; and Gareth's eyes had flying blots
Before them when he turn'd from watching
 him.
He from beyond the roaring shallow roar'd,
"What doest thou, brother, in my marches
 here?"
And she athwart the shallow shrill'd again,
"Here is a kitchen-knave from Arthur's hall
Hath overthrown thy brother, and hath his
 arms."
"Ugh!" cried the Sun, and vizoring up a red
And cipher face of rounded foolishness,
Push'd horse across the foamings of the ford,

Whom Gareth met midstream; no room was there
For lance or tourney-skill: four strokes they struck
With sword, and these were mighty; the new knight
Had fear he might be shamed; but as the Sun
Heaved up a ponderous arm to strike the fifth,
The hoof of his horse slipt in the stream, the stream
Descended, and the Sun was wash'd away.

Then Gareth laid his lance athwart the ford;

So drew him home; but he that fought no
    more,
As being all bone-batter'd on the rock,
Yielded; and Gareth sent him to the King.
"Myself when I return will plead for thee.
Lead, and I follow." Quietly she led.
"Hath not the good wind, damsel, changed
    again?"
"Nay, not a point: nor art thou victor here.
There lies a ridge of slate across the ford;
His horse thereon stumbled—ay, for I saw it.

"'O Sun' (not this strong fool whom thou, Sir
    Knave,
Hast overthrown thro' mere unhappiness),
'O Sun, that wakenest all to bliss or pain,

O moon, that layest all to sleep again,
Shine sweetly: twice my love hath smiled on
  me.'

"What knowest thou of lovesong or of
  love?
Nay, nay, God wot, so thou wert nobly born,
Thou hast a pleasant presence. Yea, perchance,——

"'O dewy flowers that open to the sun,
O dewy flowers that close when day is done,
Blow sweetly: twice my love hath smiled on me.'

"What knowest thou of flowers, except, belike,

To garnish meats with? hath not our good
 King
Who lent me thee, the flower of kitchendom,
A foolish love for flowers? what stick ye round
The pasty? wherewithal deck the boar's head?
Flowers? nay, the boar hath rosemaries and
 bay.

" 'O birds, that warble to the morning sky,
O birds that warble as the day goes by,
Sing sweetly; twice my love hath smiled on
 me.'

"What knowest thou of birds, lark, mavis,
 merle,
Linnet? what dream ye when they utter forth

May-music growing with the growing light,
Their sweet sun-worship? these be for the snare
(So runs thy fancy) these be for the spit,
Larding and basting. See thou have not now
Larded thy last, except thou turn and fly.
There stands the third fool of their allegory."

For there beyond a bridge of treble bow,
All in a rose-red from the west, and all
Naked it seem'd, and glowing in the broad
Deep-dimpled current underneath, the knight,
That named himself the Star of Evening,
    stood.

And Gareth, "Wherefore waits the madman
    there

Naked in open dayshine?" "Nay," she cried,
"Not naked, only wrapt in harden'd skins
That fit him like his own; and so ye cleave
His armour off him, these will turn the blade."

Then the third brother shouted o'er the
    bridge,
"O brother-star, why shine ye here so low?
Thy ward is higher up: but have ye slain
The damsel's champion?" and the damsel
    cried,

"No star of thine, but shot from Arthur's
    heaven
With all disaster unto thine and thee!
For both thy younger brethren have gone down

Before this youth; and so wilt thou, Sir Star;
Art thou not old?"

"Old, damsel, old and hard,
Old, with the might and breath of twenty
    boys."
Said Gareth, "Old, and over-bold in brag!
But that same strength which threw the Morning-
    Star
Can throw the Evening."

Then that other blew
A hard and deadly note upon the horn.
"Approach and arm me!" With slow steps from
    out
An old storm-beaten, russet, many-stain'd

Pavilion, forth a grizzled damsel came,
And arm'd him in old arms, and brought a helm
With but a drying evergreen for crest,
And gave a shield whereon the Star of Even
Half-tarnish'd and half-bright, his emblem, shone.
But when it glitter'd o'er the saddle-bow,
They madly hurl'd together on the bridge;
And Gareth overthrew him, lighted, drew,
There met him drawn, and overthrew him again,
But up like fire he started: and as oft
As Gareth brought him grovelling on his knees,
So many a time he vaulted up again;
Till Gareth panted hard, and his great heart,

Foredooming all his trouble was in vain,
Labour'd within him, for he seem'd as one
That all in later, sadder age begins
To war against ill uses of a life,
But these from all his life arise, and cry,
"Thou hast made us lords, and canst not put us
   down!"
He half despairs; so Gareth seem'd to strike
Vainly, the damsel clamouring all the while,
"Well done, knave-knight, well-stricken, O good
   knight-knave—
O knave, as noble as any of all the knights—
Shame me not, shame me not. I have
   prophesied—
Strike, thou art worthy of the Table Round—
His arms are old, he trusts the harden'd skin—

Strike — strike — the wind will never change
again."
And Gareth hearing ever stronglier smote,
And hew'd great pieces of his armour off him,
But lash'd in vain against the harden'd skin,
And could not wholly bring him under, more
Than loud Southwesterns, rolling ridge on
ridge,
The buoy that rides at sea, and dips and
springs
For ever; till at length Sir Gareth's brand
Clash'd his, and brake it utterly to the hilt.
"I have thee now;" but forth that other
sprang,
And, all unknightlike, writhed his wiry arms
Around him, till he felt, despite his mail,

Strangled, but straining ev'n his uttermost
Cast, and so hurl'd him headlong o'er the bridge
Down to the river, sink or swim, and cried,
"Lead, and I follow."

      But the damsel said,
"I lead no longer; ride thou at my side;
Thou art the kingliest of all kitchen-knaves.

"'O trefoil, sparkling on the rainy plain,
O rainbow with three colours after rain,
Shine sweetly: thrice my love hath smiled on
  me.'

"Sir—and, good faith, I fain had added—
  Knight,

But that I heard thee call thyself a knave,—
Shamed am I that I so rebuked, reviled,
Missaid thee; noble I am; and thought the
    King
Scorn'd me and mine; and now thy pardon,
    friend,
For thou hast ever answer'd courteously,
And wholly bold thou art, and meek withal
As any of Arthur's best, but, being knave,
Hast mazed my wit: I marvel what thou art."

"Damsel," he said, "ye be not all to blame,
Saving that ye mistrusted our good King
Would handle scorn, or yield thee, asking,
    one
Not fit to cope thy quest. Ye said your say;

Mine answer was my deed. Good sooth! I
    hold
He scarce is knight, yea but half-man, nor
    meet
To fight for gentle damsel, he, who lets
His heart be stirr'd with any foolish heat
At any gentle damsel's waywardness.
Shamed! care not! thy foul sayings fought for
    me:
And seeing now thy words are fair, methinks,
There rides no knight, not Lancelot, his great
    self,
Hath force to quell me."

                  Nigh upon that hour
When the lone hern forgets his melancholy,

Lets down his other leg, and stretching, dreams
Of goodly supper in the distant pool,
Then turn'd the noble damsel smiling at him,
And told him of a cavern hard at hand,
Where bread and baken meats and good red wine
Of Southland, which the Lady Lyonors
Had sent her coming champion, waited him.

Anon they past a narrow comb wherein
Were slabs of rock with figures, knights on horse
Sculptured, and deckt in slowly-waning hues.
"Sir Knave, my knight, a hermit once was here,

Whose holy hand hath fashion'd on the rock
The war of Time against the soul of man.
And yon four fools have suck'd their allegory
From these damp walls, and taken but the form.
Know ye not these?" and Gareth lookt and read—
In letters like to those the vexillary
Hath left crag-carven o'er the streaming Gelt—
"PHOSPHORUS," then "MERIDIES"—"HESPERUS"—
"Nox"—"MORS," beneath five figures, armed men,
Slab after slab, their faces forward all,
And running down the Soul, a Shape that fled

With broken wings, torn raiment and loose
       hair,
For help and shelter to the hermit's cave.
"Follow the faces, and we find it. Look,
Who comes behind?"

                        For one—delay'd at first
Thro' helping back the dislocated Kay
To Camelot, then by what thereafter chanced,
The damsel's headlong error thro' the wood—
Sir Lancelot, having swum the river-loops—
His blue shield-lions cover'd—softly drew
Behind the twain, and when he saw the star
Gleam, on Sir Gareth's turning to him, cried,
"Stay, felon knight, I avenge me for my
       friend."

And Gareth crying prick'd against the cry;
But when they closed—in a moment—at one touch
Of that skill'd spear, the wonder of the world—
Went sliding down so easily, and fell,
That when he found the grass within his hands
He laugh'd; the laughter jarr'd upon Lynette:
Harshly she ask'd him, "Shamed and overthrown,
And tumbled back into the kitchen-knave,
Why laugh ye? that ye blew your boast in vain?"
"Nay, noble damsel, but that I, the son

Of old King Lot and good Queen Bellicent,
And victor of the bridges and the ford,
And knight of Arthur, here lie thrown by whom
I know not, all thro' mere unhappiness—
Device and sorcery and unhappiness—
Out, sword; we are thrown!" And Lancelot
answer'd, "Prince,
O Gareth—thro' the mere unhappiness
Of one who came to help thee not to harm,
' Lancelot, and all as glad to find thee whole,
As on the day when Arthur knighted him."

Then Gareth, "Thou—Lancelot!—thine the hand
That threw me? An some chance to mar the boast

Thy brethren of thee make—which could not
        chance—
Had sent thee down before a lesser spear,
Shamed had I been and sad—O Lancelot—
        thou!"

Whereat the maiden, petulant, "Lancelot,
Why came ye not, when call'd? and wherefore
        now
Come ye, not call'd? I gloried in my knave,
Who being still rebuked, would answer still
Courteous as any knight—but now, if knight,
The marvel dies, and leaves me fool'd and
        trick'd,
And only wondering wherefore play'd upon:
And doubtful whether I and mine be scorn'd.

Where should be truth if not in Arthur's hall,
In Arthur's presence? Knight, knave, prince and
    fool,
I hate thee and for ever."

                        And Lancelot said,
"Blessed be thou, Sir Gareth! knight art thou
To the King's best wish. O damsel, be ye
    wise
To call him shamed, who is but overthrown?
Thrown have I been, nor once, but many a
    time.
Victor from vanquish'd issues at the last,
And overthrower from being overthrown.
With sword we have not striven; and thy good
    horse

And thou are weary; yet not less I felt
Thy manhood thro' that wearied lance of thine.
Well hast thou done; for all the stream is
    freed,
And thou hast wreak'd his justice on his foes,
And when reviled, hast answer'd graciously,
And makest merry, when overthrown. Prince,
    Knight,
Hail, Knight and Prince, and of our Table
    Round!"

And then when turning to Lynette he told
The tale of Gareth, petulantly she said,
"Ay well — ay well — for worse than being
    fool'd
Of others, is to fool one's self. A cave,

Sir Lancelot, is hard by, with meats and
    drinks
And forage for the horse, and flint for fire.
But all about it flies a honeysuckle.
Seek, till we find." And when they sought and
    found,
Sir Gareth drank and ate, and all his life
Past into sleep; on whom the maiden gazed.
"Sound sleep be thine! sound cause to sleep hast
    thou.
Wake lusty! Seem I not as tender to him
As any mother? Ay, but such a one
As all day long hath rated at her child,
And vext his day, but blesses him asleep—
Good lord, how sweetly smells the honey-
    suckle

In the hush'd night, as if the world were one
Of utter peace, and love, and gentleness!
O Lancelot, Lancelot" — and she clapt her
            hands —
"Full merry am I to find my goodly knave
Is knight and noble. See now, sworn have I,
Else yon black felon had not let me pass,
To bring thee back to do the battle with him.
Thus an thou goest, he will fight thee first;
Who doubts thee victor? so will my knight-
            knave
Miss the full flower of this accomplishment."

    Said Lancelot, "Peradventure he, ye name,
May know my shield. Let Gareth, an he will,
Change his for mine, and take my charger, fresh,

Not to be spurr'd, loving the battle as well
As he that rides him." "Lancelot-like," she said,
"Courteous in this, Lord Lancelot, as in all."

And Gareth, wakening, fiercely clutch'd the shield;
"Ramp ye lance-splintering lions, on whom all spears
Are rotten sticks! ye seem agape to roar!
Yea, ramp and roar at leaving of your lord!—
Care not, good beasts, so well I care for you.
O noble Lancelot, from my hold on these
Streams virtue—fire—thro' one that will not shame

Even the shadow of Lancelot under shield.
Hence; let us go."

                Silent the silent field
They traversed. Arthur's harp tho' summer-wan,
In counter motion to the clouds, allured
The glance of Gareth dreaming on his liege.
A star shot: "Lo," said Gareth, "the foe falls!"
An owl whoopt: "Hark the victor pealing there!"
Suddenly she that rode upon his left
Clung to the shield that Lancelot lent him, crying,
"Yield, yield him this again: 'tis he must fight;

I curse the tongue that all thro' yesterday
Reviled thee, and hath wrought on Lancelot now
To lend thee horse and shield: wonders ye have done;
Miracles ye cannot: here is glory enow
In having flung the three: I see thee maim'd,
Mangled: I swear thou canst not fling the fourth."

"And wherefore, damsel? tell me all ye know.
Ye cannot scare me; nor rough face, or voice,
Brute bulk of limb, or boundless savagery
Appal me from the quest."

"Nay, Prince," she cried,
"God wot, I never look'd upon the face,
Seeing he never rides abroad by day;
But watch'd him have I like a phantom pass
Chilling the night: nor have I heard the
    voice.
Always he made his mouthpiece of a page
Who came and went, and still reported him
As closing in himself the strength of ten,
And when his anger tare him, massacring
Man, woman, lad and girl—yea, the soft
    babe!
Some hold that he hath swallow'd infant flesh,
Monster! O prince, I went for Lancelot first,
The quest is Lancelot's: give him back the
    shield."

Said Gareth laughing, "An he fight for this,
Belike he wins it as the better man:
Thus—and not else?"

      But Lancelot on him urged
All the devisings of their chivalry
Where one might meet a mightier than himself;
How best to manage horse, lance, sword and
  shield,
And so fill up the gap where force might fail
With skill and fineness. Instant were his
  words.

Then Gareth, "Here be rules. I know but
  one—
To dash against mine enemy and to win.

Yet have I watch'd thee victor in the joust,
And seen thy way." "Heaven help thee," sigh'd
      Lynette.

   Then for a space, and under cloud that
      grew
To thunder-gloom palling all stars, they rode
In converse till she made her palfrey halt,
Lifted an arm, and softly whisper'd, "There."
And all the three were silent seeing, pitch'd
Beside the Castle Perilous on flat field,
A huge pavilion like a mountain peak
Sunder the glooming crimson on the marge,
Black, with black banner, and a long black
      horn
Beside it hanging; which Sir Gareth graspt,

And so, before the two could hinder him,
Sent all his heart and breath thro' all the
  horn.
Echo'd the walls; a light twinkled; anon
Came lights and lights, and once again he
  blew;
Whereon were hollow tramplings up and
  down
And muffled voices heard, and shadows past;
Till high above him, circled with her maids,
The Lady Lyonors at a window stood,
Beautiful among lights, and waving to him
White hands, and courtesy; but when the
  Prince
Three times had blown—after long hush—at
  last—

The huge pavilion slowly yielded up,
Thro' those black foldings, that which housed therein.
High on a nightblack horse, in nightblack arms,
With white breast-bone, and barren ribs of Death,
And crown'd with fleshless laughter—some ten steps—
In the half-light—thro' the dim dawn—advanced
The monster, and then paused, and spake no word.

But Gareth spake and all indignantly,
"Fool, for thou hast, men say, the strength of ten,
Canst thou not trust the limbs thy God hath given,

But must, to make the terror of thee more,
Trick thyself out in ghastly imageries
Of that which Life hath done with, and the clod,
Less dull than thou, will hide with mantling flowers
As if for pity?" But he spake no word;
Which set the horror higher: a maiden swoon'd;
The Lady Lyonors wrung her hands and wept,
As doom'd to be the bride of Night and Death;
Sir Gareth's head prickled beneath his helm;
And ev'n Sir Lancelot thro' his warm blood felt
Ice strike, and all that mark'd him were aghast.

At once Sir Lancelot's charger fiercely
neigh'd—
At once the black horse bounded forward with
him.
Then those that did not blink the terror, saw
That Death was cast to ground, and slowly
rose.
But with one stroke Sir Gareth split the skull.
Half fell to right and half to left and lay.
Then with a stronger buffet he clove the helm
As throughly as the skull; and out from this
Issued the bright face of a blooming boy
Fresh as a flower new-born, and crying,
"Knight,
Slay me not: my three brethren bad me do it,
To make a horror all about the house,

And stay the world from Lady Lyonors.

They never dream'd the passes would be past."

Answer'd Sir Gareth graciously to one

Not many a moon his younger, "My fair child,

What madness made thee challenge the chief knight

Of Arthur's hall?" "Fair Sir, they bad me do it.

They hate the King, and Lancelot, the King's friend,

They hoped to slay him somewhere on the stream,

They never dream'd the passes could be past."

Then sprang the happier day from under-
ground;
And Lady Lyonors and her house, with dance
And revel and song, made merry over Death,
As being after all their foolish fears
And horrors only proven a blooming boy.
So large mirth lived and Gareth won the
quest.

And he that told the tale in older times
Says that Sir Gareth wedded Lyonors,
But he, that told it later, says Lynette.

THE LAST TOURNAMENT.

THE LAST TOURNAMENT.

DAGONET, the fool, whom Gawain in his mood
Had made mock-knight of Arthur's Table Round,
At Camelot, high above the yellowing woods,
Danced like a wither'd leaf before the hall.
And toward him from the hall, with harp in hand,
And from the crown thereof a carcanet
Of ruby swaying to and fro, the prize

Of Tristram in the jousts of yesterday,
Came Tristram, saying, "Why skip ye so, Sir
    Fool?"

　　For Arthur and Sir Lancelot riding once
Far down beneath a winding wall of rock
Heard a child wail. A stump of oak half-
    dead,
From roots like some black coil of carven
    snakes
Clutch'd at the crag, and started thro' mid air,
Bearing an eagle's nest: and thro' the tree
Rush'd ever a rainy wind, and thro' the wind
Pierced ever a child's cry: and crag and tree
Scaling, Sir Lancelot from the perilous nest,
This ruby necklace thrice around her neck,

And all unscarr'd from beak or talon, brought
A maiden babe; which Arthur pitying took,
Then gave it to his Queen to rear: the Queen
But coldly acquiescing, in her white arms
Received, and after loved it tenderly,
And named it Nestling; so forgot herself
A moment, and her cares; till that young life
Being smitten in mid heaven with mortal cold
Past from her; and in time the carcanet
Vext her with plaintive memories of the child:
So she, delivering it to Arthur, said,
"Take thou the jewels of this dead innocence,
And make them, an thou wilt, a tourney-prize."

To whom the King, "Peace to thine eagle-
borne

Dead nestling, and this honour after death,
Following thy will! but, O my Queen, I muse
Why ye not wear on arm, or neck, or zone
Those diamonds that I rescued from the tarn,
And Lancelot won, methought, for thee to wear."

"Would rather ye had let them fall," she cried,
"Plunge and be lost—ill-fated as they were,
A bitterness to me!—ye look amazed,
Not knowing they were lost as soon as given—
Slid from my hands, when I was leaning out
Above the river—that unhappy child
Past in her barge: but rosier luck will go
With these rich jewels, seeing that they came

Not from the skeleton of a brother-slayer,
But the sweet body of a maiden babe.
Perchance—who knows?—the purest of thy
 knights
May win them for the purest of my maids."

She ended, and the cry of a great jousts
With trumpet-blowings ran on all the ways
From Camelot in among the faded fields
To furthest towers; and everywhere the
 knights
Arm'd for a day of glory before the King.

But on the hither side of that loud morn
Into the hall stagger'd, his visage ribb'd
From ear to ear with dogwhip-weals, his nose

Bridge-broken, one eye out, and one hand off,
And one with shatter'd fingers dangling lame,
A churl, to whom indignantly the King,

"My churl, for whom Christ died, what evil beast
Hath drawn his claws athwart thy face? or fiend?
Man was it who marr'd heaven's image in thee thus?"

Then, sputtering thro' the hedge of splinter'd teeth
Yet strangers to the tongue, and with blunt stump
Pitch-blacken'd sawing the air, said the maim'd churl,

"He took them and he drave them to his
    tower—
Some hold he was a table-knight of thine—
A hundred goodly ones—the Red Knight, he—
Lord, I was tending swine, and the Red
    Knight
Brake in upon me and drave them to his
    tower;
And when I call'd upon thy name as one
That doest right by gentle and by churl,
Maim'd me and maul'd, and would outright have
    slain,
Save that he sware me to a message, saying,
'Tell thou the King and all his liars, that I
Have founded my Round Table in the North,
And whatsoever his own knights have sworn

My knights have sworn the counter to it—and
    say
My tower is full of harlots, like his court,
But mine are worthier, seeing they profess
To be none other than themselves—and say
My knights are all adulterers like his own,
But mine are truer, seeing they profess
To be none other; and say his hour is come,
The heathen are upon him, his long lance
Broken, and his Excalibur a straw.'"

Then Arthur turn'd to Kay the seneschal,
"Take thou my churl, and tend him curiously
Like a king's heir, till all his hurts be whole.
The heathen—but that ever-climbing wave,
Hurl'd back again so often in empty foam,

Hath lain for years at rest—and renegades,
Thieves, bandits, leavings of confusion, whom
The wholesome realm is purged of other-
   where,—
Friends, thro' your manhood and your fealty,—
   now
Make their last head like Satan in the North.
My younger knights, new-made, in whom your
   flower
Waits to be solid fruit of golden deeds,
Move with me toward their quelling, which
   achieved,
The loneliest ways are safe from shore to
   shore.
But thou, Sir Lancelot, sitting in my place
Enchair'd to-morrow, arbitrate the field;

For wherefore shouldst thou care to mingle
    with it,
Only to yield my Queen her own again?
Speak, Lancelot, thou art silent: is it well?"

Thereto Sir Lancelot answer'd, "It is well:
Yet better if the King abide, and leave
The leading of his younger knights to me.
Else, for the King has will'd it, it is well."

Then Arthur rose and Lancelot follow'd
    him,
And while they stood without the doors, the
    King
Turn'd to him saying, "Is it then so well?
Or mine the blame that oft I seem as he

Of whom was written, 'A sound is in his
    ears'—
The foot that loiters, bidden go,—the glance
That only seems half-loyal to command,—
A manner somewhat fall'n from reverence—
Or have I dream'd the bearing of our knights
Tells of a manhood ever less and lower?
Or whence the fear lest this my realm, up-
    rear'd,
By noble deeds at one with noble vows,
From flat confusion and brute violences,
Reel back into the beast, and be no more?"

    He spoke, and taking all his younger
        knights,
Down the slope city rode, and sharply turn'd

North by the gate. In her high bower the
        Queen,
Working a tapestry, lifted up her head,
Watch'd her lord pass, and knew not that she
        sigh'd.
Then ran across her memory the strange rhyme
Of bygone Merlin, "Where is he who knows?
From the great deep to the great deep he
        goes."

But when the morning of a tournament,
By these in earnest those in mockery call'd
The Tournament of the Dead Innocence,
Brake with a wet wind blowing, Lancelot,
Round whose sick head all night, like birds of
        prey,

The words of Arthur flying shriek'd, arose,
And down a streetway hung with folds of
    pure
White samite, and by fountains running wine,
Where children sat in white with cups of gold,
Moved to the lists, and there, with slow sad
    steps
Ascending, fill'd his double-dragon'd chair.

He glanced and saw the stately galleries,
Dame, damsel, each thro' worship of their
    Queen
White-robed in honour of the stainless child,
And some with scatter'd jewels, like a bank
Of maiden snow mingled with sparks of fire.
He look'd but once, and vail'd his eyes again.

The sudden trumpet sounded as in a dream
To ears but half-awaked, then one low roll
Of Autumn thunder, and the jousts began:
And ever the wind blew, and yellowing leaf
And gloom and gleam, and shower and shorn
   plume
Went down it. Sighing weariedly, as one
Who sits and gazes on a faded fire,
When all the goodlier guests are past away,
Sat their great umpire, looking o'er the lists.
He saw the laws that ruled the tournament
Broken, but spake not; once, a knight cast
   down
Before his throne of arbitration cursed
The dead babe and the follies of the King;
And once the laces of a helmet crack'd,

And show'd him, like a vermin in its hole,

Modred, a narrow face: anon he heard

The voice that billow'd round the barriers roar

An ocean-sounding welcome to one knight,

But newly-enter'd, taller than the rest,

And armour'd all in forest green, whereon

There tript a hundred tiny silver deer,

And wearing but a holly-spray for crest,

With ever-scattering berries, and on shield

A spear, a harp, a bugle—Tristram—late

From overseas in Brittany return'd,

And marriage with a princess of that realm,

Isolt the White—Sir Tristram of the Woods—

Whom Lancelot knew, had held sometime with
   pain

His own against him, and now yearn'd to shake

The burthen off his heart in one full shock
With Tristram ev'n to death: his strong hands gript
And dinted the gilt dragons right and left,
Until he groan'd for wrath—so many of those,
That ware their ladies' colours on the casque,
Drew from before Sir Tristram to the bounds,
And there with gibes and flickering mockeries
Stood, while he mutter'd, "Craven crests! O shame
What faith have these in whom they sware to love?
The glory of our Round Table is no more."

So Tristram won, and Lancelot gave, the gems,

Not speaking other word than "Hast thou won?
Art thou the purest, brother? See, the hand
Wherewith thou takest this, is red!" to whom
Tristram, half plagued by Lancelot's languorous
          mood,
Made answer, "Ay, but wherefore toss me this
Like a dry bone cast to some hungry hound?
Let be thy fair Queen's fantasy. Strength of
          heart
And might of limb, but mainly use and skill,
Are winners in this pastime of our King.
My hand—belike the lance hath dript upon it—
No blood of mine, I trow; but O chief knight,
Right arm of Arthur in the battlefield,
Great brother, thou nor I have made the world;
Be happy in thy fair Queen as I in mine."

And Tristram round the gallery made his
    horse
Caracole; then bow'd his homage, bluntly
    saying,
"Fair damsels, each to him who worships each
Sole Queen of Beauty and of love, behold
This day my Queen of Beauty is not here."
And most of these were mute, some anger'd,
    one
Murmuring, "All courtesy is dead," and one,
"The glory of our Round Table is no more."

Then fell thick rain, plume droopt and mantle
    clung,
And pettish cries awoke, and the wan day
Went glooming down in wet and weariness:

THE LAST TOURNAMENT.

But under her black brows a swarthy one

Laugh'd shrilly, crying, "Praise the patient saints,

Our one white day of Innocence hath past,

Tho' somewhat draggled at the skirt. So be it.

The snowdrop only, flowering thro' the year,

Would make the world as blank as winter-tide.

Come — let us gladden their sad eyes, our Queen's

And Lancelot's, at this night's solemnity

With all the kindlier colours of the field."

So dame and damsel glitter'd at the feast

Variously gay: for he that tells the tale

Liken'd them, saying, as when an hour of cold

Falls on the mountain in midsummer snows,
And all the purple slopes of mountain flowers
Pass under white, till the warm hour returns
With veer of wind, and all are flowers again;
So dame and damsel cast the simple white,
And glowing in all colours, the live grass,
Rose-campion, bluebell, kingcup, poppy, glanced
About the revels, and with mirth so loud
Beyond all use, that, half-amazed, the Queen,
And wroth at Tristram and the lawless jousts,
Brake up their sports, then slowly to her bower
Parted, and in her bosom pain was lord.

And little Dagonet on the morrow morn,
High over all the yellowing Autumn-tide,

Danced like a wither'd leaf before the hall.

Then Tristram saying, "Why skip ye so, Sir
 Fool?"

Wheel'd round on either heel, Dagonet replied,

"Belike for lack of wiser company;

Or being fool, and seeing too much wit

Makes the world rotten, why, belike I skip

To know myself the wisest knight of all."

"Ay, fool," said Tristram, "but 'tis eating dry

To dance without a catch, a roundelay

To dance to." Then he twangled on his
 harp,

And while he twangled little Dagonet stood,

Quiet as any water-sodden log

Stay'd in the wandering warble of a brook;

But when the twangling ended, skipt again;

Then being ask'd, "Why skipt ye not, Sir Fool?"
Made answer, "I had liefer twenty years
Skip to the broken music of my brains
Than any broken music ye can make."
Then Tristram, waiting for the quip to come,
"Good now, what music have I broken, fool?"
And little Dagonet, skipping, "Arthur, the king's;
For when thou playest that air with Queen Isolt,
Thou makest broken music with thy bride,
Her daintier namesake down in Brittany—
And so thou breakest Arthur's music too."
"Save for that broken music in thy brains,
Sir Fool," said Tristram, "I would break thy head.

Fool, I came late, the heathen wars were o'er,
The life had flown, we sware but by the
    shell —
I am but a fool to reason with a fool —
Come, thou art crabb'd and sour: but lean me
    down,
Sir Dagonet, one of thy long asses' ears,
And harken if my music be not true.

"'Free love — free field — we love but while
    we may:
The woods are hush'd, their music is no more:
The leaf is dead, the yearning past away:
New leaf, new life — the days of frost are
    o'er:
New life, new love, to suit the newer day:

New loves are sweet as those that went before:
Free love—free field—we love but while we
may."

"Ye might have moved slow-measure to my
tune,
Not stood stockstill. I made it in the woods,
And heard it ring as true as tested gold."

But Dagonet with one foot poised in his
hand,
"Friend, did ye mark that fountain yesterday
Made to run wine?—but this had run itself
All out like a long life to a sour end—
And them that round it sat with golden cups
To hand the wine to whosoever came—

The twelve small damosels white as Innocence,
In honour of poor Innocence the babe,
Who left the gems which Innocence the Queen
Lent to the King, and Innocence the King
Gave for a prize—and one of those white slips
Handed her cup and piped, the pretty one,
'Drink, drink, Sir Fool,' and thereupon I
    drank,
Spat – pish—the cup was gold, the draught was
    mud."

And Tristram, "Was it muddier than thy
    gibes?
Is all the laughter gone dead out of thee?—
Not marking how the knighthood mock thee,
    fool—

'Fear God: honour the king — his one true knight—
Sole follower of the vows'—for here be they
Who knew thee swine enow before I came,
Smuttier than blasted grain: but when the King
Had made thee fool, thy vanity so shot up
It frighted all free fool from out thy heart;
Which left thee less than fool, and less than swine,
A naked aught—yet swine I hold thee still,
For I have flung thee pearls and find thee swine."

And little Dagonet mincing with his feet,
"Knight, an ye fling those rubies round my neck

In lieu of hers, I'll hold thou hast some touch
Of music, since I care not for thy pearls.
Swine? I have wallow'd, I have wash'd—the
    world
Is flesh and shadow—I have had my day.
The dirty nurse, Experience, in her kind
Hath foul'd me—an I wallow'd, then I
    wash'd—
I have had my day and my philosophies—
And thank the Lord I am King Arthur's fool.
Swine, say ye? swine, goats, asses, rams and
    geese
Troop'd round a Paynim harper once, who
    thrumm'd
On such a wire as musically as thou
Some such fine song--but never a king's fool."

And Tristram, "Then were swine, goats, asses, geese
The wiser fools, seeing thy Paynim bard
Had such a mastery of his mystery
That he could harp his wife up out of hell."

Then Dagonet, turning on the ball of his foot,
"And whither harp'st thou thine? down! and thyself
Down! and two more: a helpful harper thou,
That harpest downward! Dost thou know the star
We call the harp of Arthur up in heaven?"

And Tristram, "Ay, Sir Fool, for when our King
Was victor wellnigh day by day, the knights,
Glorying in each new glory, set his name
High on all hills, and in the signs of heaven."

And Dagonet answer'd, "Ay, and when the land
Was freed, and the Queen false, ye set yourself
To babble about him, all to show your wit—
And whether he were king by courtesy,
Or king by right—and so went harping down
The black king's highway, got so far, and grew
So witty that ye play'd at ducks and drakes

With Arthur's vows on the great lake of fire.
Tuwhoo! do ye see it? do ye see the star?"

"Nay, fool," said Tristram, "not in open
  day."
And Dagonet, "Nay, nor will: I see it and
  hear.
It makes a silent music up in heaven,
And I, and Arthur and the angels hear,
And then we skip." "Lo, fool," he said, "ye
  talk
Fool's treason: is the King thy brother fool?"
Then little Dagonet clapt his hands and
  shrill'd,
"Ay, ay, my brother fool, the king of fools!
Conceits himself as God that he can make

Figs out of thistles, silk from bristles, milk
From burning spurge, honey from hornet-
　　combs,
And men from beasts—Long live the king of
　　fools!"

And down the city Dagonet danced away.
But thro' the slowly-mellowing avenues
And solitary passes of the wood
Rode Tristram toward Lyonesse and the west.
Before him fled the face of Queen Isolt
With ruby-circled neck, but evermore
Past, as a rustle or twitter in the wood
Made dull his inner, keen his outer eye
For all that walk'd, or crept, or perch'd, or
　　flew.

Anon the face, as, when a gust hath blown,
Unruffling waters re-collect the shape
Of one that in them sees himself return'd;
But at the slot or fewmets of a deer,
Or ev'n a fall'n feather, vanish'd again.

So on for all that day from lawn to lawn
Thro' many a league-long bower he rode. At length
A lodge of intertwisted beechen-boughs
Furze-cramm'd, and bracken-rooft, the which himself
Built for a summer day with Queen Isolt
Against a shower, dark in the golden grove
Appearing, sent his fancy back to where
She lived a moon in that low lodge with him:

Till Mark her lord had past, the Cornish king,
With six or seven, when Tristram was away,
And snatch'd her thence; yet dreading worse than
    shame
Her warrior Tristram, spake not any word,
But bode his hour, devising wretchedness.

And now that desert lodge to Tristram
    lookt
So sweet, that halting, in he past, and sank
Down on a drift of foliage random-blown;
But could not rest for musing how to smooth
And sleek his marriage over to the Queen.
Perchance in lone Tintagil far from all
The tonguesters of the court she had not
    heard.

But then what folly had sent him overseas
After she left him lonely here? a name?
Was it the name of one in Brittany,
Isolt, the daughter of the King? "Isolt
Of the white hands" they call'd her: the sweet name
Allured him first, and then the maid herself,
Who served him well with those white hands of hers,
And loved him well, until himself had thought
He loved her also, wedded easily,
But left her all as easily, and return'd.
The black-blue Irish hair and Irish eyes
Had drawn him home—what marvel? then he laid
His brows upon the drifted leaf and dream'd.

He seem'd to pace the strand of Brittany
Between Isolt of Britain and his bride,
And show'd them both the ruby-chain, and
    both
Began to struggle for it, till his Queen
Graspt it so hard, that all her hand was red.
Then cried the Breton, "Look, her hand is
    red!
These be no rubies, this is frozen blood,
And melts within her hand—her hand is hot
With ill desires, but this I gave thee, look,
Is all as cool and white as any flower."
Follow'd a rush of eagle's wings, and then
A whimpering of the spirit of the child,
Because the twain had spoil'd her carcanet.

He dream'd; but Arthur with a hundred
    spears
Rode far, till o'er the illimitable reed,
And many a glancing plash and sallowy isle,
The wide-wing'd sunset of the misty marsh
Glared on a huge machicolated tower
That stood with open doors, whereout was roll'd
A roar of riot, as from men secure
Amid their marshes, ruffians at their ease
Among their harlot-brides, an evil song.
"Lo there," said one of Arthur's youth, for
    there,
High on a grim dead tree before the tower,
A goodly brother of the Table Round
Swung by the neck: and on the boughs a
    shield

Showing a shower of blood in a field noir,
And therebeside a horn, inflamed the knights
At that dishonour done the gilded spur,
Till each would clash the shield, and blow the
horn.

But Arthur waved them back. Alone he rode.
Then at the dry harsh roar of the great horn,
That sent the face of all the marsh aloft
An ever upward-rushing storm and cloud
Of shriek and plume, the Red Knight heard,
and all,
Even to tipmost lance and topmost helm,
In blood-red armour sallying, howl'd to the
King,
"The teeth of Hell flay bare and gnash thee
flat!

Lo! art thou not that eunuch-hearted King
Who fain had clipt free manhood from the
    world—
The woman-worshipper? Yea, God's curse, and I!
Slain was the brother of my paramour
By a knight of thine, and I that heard her
    whine
And snivel, being eunuch-hearted too,
Sware by the scorpion-worm that twists in hell,
And stings itself to everlasting death,
To hang whatever knight of thine I fought
And tumbled. Art thou King?— Look to thy
    life!"

He ended: Arthur knew the voice; the face
Wellnigh was helmet-hidden, and the name

Went wandering somewhere darkling in his
    mind.
And Arthur deign'd not use of word or sword,
But let the drunkard, as he stretch'd from horse
To strike him, overbalancing his bulk,
Down from the causeway heavily to the swamp
Fall, as the crest of some slow-arching wave,
Heard in dead night along that table-shore,
Drops flat, and after the great waters break
Whitening for half a league, and thin them-
    selves,
Far over sands marbled with moon and cloud,
From less and less to nothing; thus he fell
Head-heavy, while the knights, who watch'd him,
    roar'd
And shouted and leapt down upon the fall'n;

There trampled out his face from being known,
And sank his head in mire, and slimed themselves:
Nor heard the King for their own cries, but sprang
Thro' open doors, and swording right and left
Men, women, on their sodden faces, hurl'd
The tables over and the wines, and slew
Till all the rafters rang with woman-yells,
And all the pavement stream'd with massacre:
Then, yell with yell echoing, they fired the tower,
Which half that autumn night, like the live North,
Red-pulsing up thro' Alioth and Alcor,
Made all above it, and a hundred meres

About it, as the water Moab saw
Come round by the East, and out beyond them
    flush'd
The long low dune, and lazy-plunging sea.

So all the ways were safe from shore to
    shore,
But in the heart of Arthur pain was lord.

Then, out of Tristram waking, the red dream
Fled with a shout, and that low lodge return'd,
Mid-forest, and the wind among the boughs.
He whistled his good warhorse left to graze
Among the forest greens, vaulted upon him,
And rode beneath an ever-showering leaf,
Till one lone woman, weeping near a cross,

Stay'd him. "Why weep ye?" "Lord," she said,
    "my man
Hath left me or is dead;" whereon he thought—
"What, an she hate me now? I would not this.
What, an she love me still? I would not that.
I know not what I would"—but said to her,
"Yet weep not thou, lest, if thy mate return,
He find thy favour changed and love thee
    not"—
Then pressing day by day thro' Lyonesse
Last in a roky hollow, belling, heard
The hounds of Mark, and felt the goodly
    hounds
Yelp at his heart, but turning, past and gain'd
Tintagil, half in sea, and high on land,
A crown of towers.

Down in a casement sat,
A low sea-sunset glorying round her hair
And glossy-throated grace, Isolt the Queen.
And when she heard the feet of Tristram grind
The spiring stone that scaled about her tower,
Flush'd, started, met him at the doors, and there
Belted his body with her white embrace
Crying aloud, "Not Mark—not Mark, my soul!
The footstep flutter'd me at first: not he:
Catlike thro' his own castle steals my Mark,
But warrior-wise thou stridest thro' his halls
Who hates thee, as I him—ev'n to the death.
My soul, I felt my hatred for my Mark
Quicken within me, and knew that thou wert nigh."

To whom Sir Tristram smiling, "I am here.
Let be thy Mark, seeing he is not thine."

And drawing somewhat backward she replied,
"Can he be wrong'd who is not ev'n his own,
But save for dread of thee had beaten me,
Scratch'd, bitten, blinded, marr'd me somehow—
  Mark?
What rights are his that dare not strike for
  them?
Not lift a hand—not, tho' he found me thus!
But harken! have ye met him? hence he went
To-day for three days' hunting—as he said—
And so returns belike within an hour.
Mark's way, my soul!—but eat not thou with
  Mark,

Because he hates thee even more than fears;
Nor drink: and when thou passest any wood
Close vizor, lest an arrow from the bush
Should leave me all alone with Mark and hell.
My God, the measure of my hate for Mark,
Is as the measure of my love for thee."

So, pluck'd one way by hate and one by
 love,
Drain'd of her force, again she sat, and spake
To Tristram, as he knelt before her, saying,
"O hunter, and O blower of the horn,
Harper, and thou hast been a rover too,
For, ere I mated with my shambling king,
Ye twain had fallen out about the bride
Of one—his name is out of me—the prize,

If prize she were—(what marvel—she could see)—
Thine, friend; and ever since my craven seeks
To wreck thee villainously: but, O Sir Knight,
What dame or damsel have ye kneel'd to last?"

And Tristram, "Last to my Queen Paramount,
Here now to my Queen Paramount of love
And loveliness—ay, lovelier than when first
Her light feet fell on our rough Lyonesse,
Sailing from Ireland."

Softly laugh'd Isolt,
"Flatter me not, for hath not our great Queen
My dole of beauty trebled?" and he said,
"Her beauty is her beauty, and thine thine,
And thine is more to me—soft, gracious, kind—

Save when thy Mark is kindled on thy lips
Most gracious; but she, haughty, ev'n to him,
Lancelot; for I have seen him wan enow
To make one doubt if ever the great Queen
Have yielded him her love."

       To whom Isolt,
"Ah then, false hunter and false harper, thou
Who brakest thro' the scruple of my bond,
Calling me thy white hind, and saying to me
That Guinevere had sinn'd against the highest,
And I—misyoked with such a want of man—
That I could hardly sin against the lowest."

 He answer'd, "O my soul, be comforted!
If this be sweet, to sin in leading-strings,

If here be comfort, and if ours be sin,
Crown'd warrant had we for the crowning sin
That made us happy: but how ye greet me—
    fear
And fault and doubt — no word of that fond
    tale—
Thy deep heart-yearnings, thy sweet memories
Of Tristram in that year he was away."

And, saddening on the sudden, spake Isolt,
"I had forgotten all in my strong joy
To see thee — yearnings? — ay! for, hour by
    hour,
Here in the never-ended afternoon,
O sweeter than all memories of thee,
Deeper than any yearnings after thee

Seem'd those far-rolling, westward-smiling seas,
Watch'd from this tower. Isolt of Britain dash'd
Before Isolt of Brittany on the strand,
Would that have chill'd her bride-kiss? Wedded
    her?
Fought in her father's battles? wounded there?
The King was all fulfill'd with gratefulness,
And she, my namesake of the hands, that heal'd
Thy hurt and heart with unguent and caress—
Well—can I wish her any huger wrong
Than having known thee? her too hast thou
    left
To pine and waste in those sweet memories.
O were I not my Mark's, by whom all men
Are noble, I should hate thee more than
    love."

And Tristram, fondling her light hands, replied,
"Grace, Queen, for being loved: she loved me well.
Did I love her? the name at least I loved.
Isolt?—I fought his battles, for Isolt!
The night was dark; the true star set. Isolt!
The name was ruler of the dark——Isolt?
Care not for her! patient, and prayerful, meek,
Pale-blooded, she will yield herself to God."

And Isolt answer'd, "Yea, and why not I?
Mine is the larger need, who am not meek,
Pale-blooded, prayerful. Let me tell thee now.
Here one black, mute midsummer night I sat,
Lonely, but musing on thee, wondering where,

Murmuring a light song I had heard thee sing,
And once or twice I spake thy name aloud.
Then flash'd a levin-brand; and near me stood,
In fuming sulphur blue and green, a fiend—
Mark's way to steal behind one in the dark—
For there was Mark: 'He has wedded her,' he said,
Not said, but hiss'd it: then this crown of towers
So shook to such a roar of all the sky,
That here in utter dark I swoon'd away,
And woke again in utter dark, and cried,
'I will flee hence and give myself to God'—
And thou wert lying in thy new leman's arms."

Then Tristram, ever dallying with her hand,
"May God be with thee, sweet, when old and
  gray,

And past desire!" a saying that anger'd her.
"'May God be with thee, sweet, when thou art
      old,
And sweet no more to me!' I need Him now.
For when had Lancelot utter'd aught so gross
Ev'n to the swineherd's malkin in the mast?
The greater man, the greater courtesy.
But thou, thro' ever harrying thy wild beasts—
Save that to touch a harp tilt with a lance
Becomes thee well—art grown wild beast thyself.
How darest thou, if lover, push me even
In fancy from thy side, and set me far
In the gray distance, half a life away,
Her to be loved no more? Unsay it, unswear!
Flatter me rather, seeing me so weak,
Broken with Mark and hate and solitude,

Thy marriage and mine own, that I should suck
Lies like sweet wines: lie to me: I believe.
Will ye not lie? not swear, as there ye kneel,
And solemnly as when ye sware to him,
The man of men, our King—My God, the power
Was once in vows when men believed the King!
They lied not then, who sware, and thro' their
  vows
The King prevailing made his realm:—I say,
Swear to me thou wilt love me ev'n when old,
Gray-hair'd, and past desire, and in despair."

  Then Tristram, pacing moodily up and down,
"Vows! did ye keep the vow ye made to Mark
More than I mine? Lied, say ye? Nay, but
  learnt,

The vow that binds too strictly snaps itself—
My knighthood taught me this—ay, being snapt—
We run more counter to the soul thereof
Than had we never sworn. I swear no more.
I swore to the great King, and am forsworn.
For once—ev'n to the height—I honour'd him.
'Man, is he man at all?' methought, when first
I rode from our rough Lyonesse, and beheld
That victor of the Pagan throned in hall—
His hair, a sun that ray'd from off a brow
Like hillsnow high in heaven, the steel-blue eyes,
The golden beard that clothed his lips with
      light—
Moreover, that weird legend of his birth,
With Merlin's mystic babble about his end
Amazed me; then, his foot was on a stool

Shaped as a dragon; he seem'd to me no man,
But Michaël trampling Satan; so I sware,
Being amazed: but this went by—The vows!
O ay—the wholesome madness of an hour—
They served their use, their time; for every knight
Believed himself a greater than himself,
And every follower eyed him as a God;
Till he, being lifted up beyond himself,
Did mightier deeds than elsewise he had done,
And so the realm was made; but then their
    vows—
First mainly thro' that sullying of our Queen—
Began to gall the knighthood, asking whence
Had Arthur right to bind them to himself?
Dropt down from heaven? wash'd up from out
    the deep?

'They fail'd to trace him thro' the flesh and
    blood
Of our old Kings: whence then? a doubtful lord
To bind them by inviolable vows,
Which flesh and blood perforce would violate:
For feel this arm of mine—the tide within
Red with free chase and heather-scented air,
Pulsing full man; can Arthur make me pure
As any maiden child? lock up my tongue
From uttering freely what I freely hear?
Bind me to one? The wide world laughs at it.
And worldling of the world am I, and know
The ptarmigan that whitens ere his hour
Woos his own end; we are not angels here
Nor shall be: vows—I am woodman of the
    woods,

And hear the garnet-headed yaffingale
Mock them: my soul, we love but while we
may;
And therefore is my love so large for thee,
Seeing it is not bounded save by love."

Here ending, he moved toward her, and she
said,
"Good: an I turn'd away my love for thee
To some one thrice as courteous as thyself—
For courtesy wins woman all as well
As valour may, but he that closes both
Is perfect, he is Lancelot—taller indeed,
Rosier, and comelier, thou—but say I loved
This knightliest of all knights, and cast thee
back

Thine own small saw, 'We love but while we
	may,'
Well then, what answer?"

			He that while she spake,
Mindful of what he brought to adorn her with,
The jewels, had let one finger lightly touch
The warm white apple of her throat, replied,
"Press this a little closer, sweet, until—
Come, I am hunger'd and half-anger'd—meat,
Wine, wine—and I will love thee to the death,
And out beyond into the dream to come."

    So then, when both were brought to full
		accord,
She rose, and set before him all he will'd;

And after these had comforted the blood
With meats and wines, and satiated their
    hearts—
Now talking of their woodland paradise,
The deer, the dews, the fern, the founts, the
    lawns;
Now mocking at the much ungainliness,
And craven shifts, and long crane legs of
    Mark—
Then Tristram laughing caught the harp, and
    sang:

   "Ay, ay, O ay—the winds that bend the
       brier!
A star in heaven, a star within the mere!
Ay, ay, O ay—a star was my desire,

And one was far apart, and one was near:
Ay, ay, O ay—the winds that bow the grass!
And one was water and one star was fire,
And one will ever shine and one will pass.
Ay, ay, O ay—the winds that move the mere."

Then in the light's last glimmer Tristram show'd
And swung the ruby carcanet. She cried,
"The collar of some Order, which our King
Hath newly founded, all for thee, my soul,
For thee, to yield thee grace beyond thy peers."

"Not so, my Queen," he said, "but the red fruit
Grown on a magic oak-tree in mid-heaven,

And won by Tristram as a tourney-prize,
And hither brought by Tristram for his last
Love-offering and peace-offering unto thee."

He rose, he turn'd, then, flinging round her neck,
Claspt it, and cried "Thine Order, O my Queen!"
But, while he bow'd to kiss the jewell'd throat,
Out of the dark, just as the lips had touch'd,
Behind him rose a shadow and a shriek—
"Mark's way," said Mark, and clove him thro'
the brain.

That night came Arthur home, and while he climb'd,
All in a death-dumb autumn-dripping gloom

The stairway to the hall, and look'd and saw
The great Queen's bower was dark,—about his feet
A voice clung sobbing till he question'd it,
"What art thou?" and the voice about his feet
Sent up an answer, sobbing, "I am thy fool,
And I shall never make thee smile again."

END OF VOL. VII.

www.ingramcontent.com/pod-product-compliance
Lightning Source LLC
Chambersburg PA
CBHW032144160426
43197CB00008B/771